You don't have to settle for second best.
You can have what you want.

"FEW ARE MORE SKILLFUL AT HELPING
PEOPLE FREE THEIR CREATIVITY than Julia
Hastings. I have the greatest respect for her work."
—Author Leslie Kenton

"CREATIVE VISUALIZATION GIVES YOU
THE POWER TO UNLOCK YOUR OWN
POTENTIAL."
—*Options*

You Can Have
What You Want

Born in California, Julia Hastings has traveled and studied motivational techniques in the United States, France, South America and England. In recent years she has devoted her study to the art of creative visualization, which she now teaches. Hastings offers seminars and one-to-one coaching to people from all walks of life. For information on seminars and other programs by Julia Hastings, please contact:

Julia Hastings
P. O. Box 57
Haslemere, Surrey GU27 2RW England

YOU CAN
Have
WHAT YOU
Want

Julia Hastings

BERKLEY BOOKS, NEW YORK

The examples of problems and visualizations in this book are completely
general in nature and do not reflect personal disclosures from clients.

YOU CAN HAVE WHAT YOU WANT

A Berkley Book / published by arrangement with
the author

PRINTING HISTORY
Touchstone edition published 1992
Berkley trade paperback edition / September 1994

ISBN: 0-425-15826-8

BERKLEY®
Berkley Books are published by The Berkley Publishing Group,
200 Madison Avenue, New York, New York 10016.
BERKLEY and the "B" design
are trademarks belonging to Berkley Publishing Corporation.

PRINTED IN THE UNITED STATES OF AMERICA

10 9 8 7 6 5 4

CONTENTS

YOU CAN

Have

WHAT YOU

Want

You are already visualizing

CHAPTER ONE

You Have a Choice!

If you are reading a book you don't like, you can put it aside. If you go to a movie you don't enjoy, you can get up and walk out. If you're at a party and you're not having fun, you can leave early. If you're living a lifestyle that doesn't make you happy, you can do the same. The problem is you don't think so. You think you're stuck with your lot. What's more you may feel it's too late to change.

The truth is you can change your lifestyle any time you want. You do this the same way you stopped reading the book, walked out of the movie or left the party early. You acknowledge that the way you're living does not give you the pleasure you thought it would and you give yourself permission to change it. The easiest way to do this is through a process called creative visualization.

An Art You'll Enjoy

Creative visualization is the art of using your imagination to create what you want in your life. You can use creative visualization to make something happen, such as a promotion, closing a deal, improving your looks or finally achieving *that* relationship. You can use it to remove things from your life like too much stress, poor health, a job that no longer suits you or people who are making you miserable.

This all may sound too good to be true, but creative visualization works. Athletes achieve peak performance by visualizing themselves winning; golfers and tennis player visualize themselves making perfect contact with the ball. Women maintain slender, toned bodies through a "mental diet" of visualization. Cancer patients reverse their diseases by visualizing their tumors disappearing. And business managers negotiate complex contracts through creative visualization.

Visualization Started in Sport

Creative visualization first gained its name in sport when psychologist Alan Richardson tested three groups of people for performance in basketball free-throwing. For twenty days, Richardson had the first group practicing every day, the second group did not practice at all, and the third group did not practice either, but they *visualized* themselves practicing. They visualized themselves making basketball free-throws.

At the end of twenty days, Richardson tested the three groups for performance. The first group had improved twenty-four per cent, the second group had not improved at all, and the third group, the visualizers, had improved twenty-three per cent. Experiments were carried out in similar sports with similar results.

Sports people found that when they brought visualization into their practice they could improve their play dramatically. Since then creative visualization has become increasingly recognized as a valuable tool for success, not only in sport, but in every field of human activity.

You Are Already Visualizing

The first problem you'll have with creative visualization is that you'll think you can't do it. Yet you are already visualizing. If I say to you "My cat likes fish," even though I haven't told you what my cat looks like, you already have a picture of a cat in your mind.

To take another example, how often do you say, "I knew it!" when something happens the way you thought it would? "I knew I'd get one!" you claim, when you find a parking space in the center of town.

Or you may groan, "Just my luck" when you have circled and circled and still haven't found a space.

The same "I knew it" attitude holds true when you get invited to a party you wanted to attend, or for that matter when you're excluded. Without realizing it, you've been visualizing the cat, the parking space and the party.

Visualizing Is Easy

When you taste, touch, smell, feel and hear you are visualizing. You don't have to see like a photograph in your mind. By evoking your five senses you can visualize powerfully. In fact you are already doing this when you "see" yourself going to the supermarket, "taste" the cool lager you want to drink, "feel" the pleasure of a warm bath, "touch" its foamy bubbles, or "hear" the sound of the sea and "smell" the salt air of the holiday you plan to take. You unconsciously visualize whenever you anticipate doing something.

So visualizing isn't new to you. It's just not conscious. *Creative visualization will teach you how to consciously do what you are already doing to create what you want in your life.*

Visualizing Is Healthy

Medical research has shown that what you look at influences your mood and your health. In less than one hundredth of a second your entire body chemistry changes when you look at something new. If you look at a sunset you produce endorphins, the hormones in your body that make you feel relaxed and at ease. If you look at a traffic jam or a violent scene you produce stress hormones that make you feel aggressive and fearful and put a strain on your body.

Give Up Worry

Worry takes a heavy toll on you. It makes you feel heavy, makes you come across heavy and sabotages your opportunities. When you worry you're no different from a salesman who comes to your door and says, "I want you to buy my product but it's no good." This is how you come across when you worry. Also people don't enjoy being around you because you're not much fun. You know this but you worry anyway. Why?

By worrying you think you can make things happen.

You think that if you watch and analyze the negative points of a situation, you can stop them from happening. This sometimes holds true, but you can alienate a lot of friendly people along the way with your pessimism and suspicion. Worry also turns achieving what you want into a struggle, instead of the enjoyable experience it should be.

Another reason you take a pessimistic attitude is to maintain a safety net: you won't feel let down when things don't work out. You may have become so accustomed to not getting what you want that you're used to settling for second best.

Focus On What You Want

Good things happen in your life when you focus on them. Disagreeable things stop happening in your life when you stop focusing on them. Your happiness, your health and your prosperity depend on your willingness to use your imagination to focus on what you want. This is the art of creative visualization. It's also the way you take your dreams out of the realm of wishful thinking and turn them into a reality.

Imagine

- What do you want?
- Close your eyes and imagine that you have it. Hear it, taste it, touch it, feel it, smell it.

- How do you feel?

- Now that you have what you want, how would your life be different?

- How would you handle the difficult people and problems in your life now that you have what you want?

Turn Your Luck Around

What creative visualization teaches you is how to be lucky. It does this by changing the negative beliefs you have about yourself that make you unlucky. You may think luck comes from the outside, but it doesn't, it comes from within. Creative visualization teaches you how to *recognize* your good luck. It's also a process that will put you firmly in control of your life and make you deeply happy as a result.

Visualizing is an effortless process

CHAPTER TWO

The Mechanics

The purpose of this book is to show you how to visualize by giving you examples you can use right away to create what you want. *There's no right way to visualize, there's only the way that feels right to you.* This is how it's done.

Techniques of creative visualization fall into three categories, those that 1) *create* what you want for yourself and others, 2) *destroy* what you don't want, and 3) *back up* your success. They can be used to improve your relationships, your career, your looks and your health.

When you visualize you go through an effortless process where you 1) *decide* what you want, 2) *relax* your mind and body, 3) *visualize* what you want in a way that implies you already have it, 4) *come out* of your visualizing, 5) *affirm* that you have what you want, 6) *act as if* you have it, and then 7) *follow through* with the actions that will make it happen.

Seeing Is Believing

Without realizing it you may be programming yourself with, "I want, I want, I want, but I haven't got."

The mental conversations you carry on with yourself can block everything you deeply desire. As you look out your window at your battered old car and sigh, "I wish I had a new car," you confirm that you haven't got one. You dream of being thin, but you look in the mirror and confirm you're still fat. You want to be wealthy but you see yourself as poor. You long for companionship but see yourself alone.

Creative visualization will teach you how to see differently. It will show you how to see in your imagination. This can profoundly change you. Every time you see what you want in your imagination, if only for a moment, what you want becomes real to you, and you're never quite the same again.

You've opened the door of possibility. Some people call it getting their juices flowing. The more you visualize what you want, the more real your wish becomes until it turns into determination. This attitude—this determination—automatically creates the opportunities you want.

Feeling Is the Secret

You'll probably find your feelings are a powerful tool in getting results fast. I've had people tell me that within five minutes after visualizing powerfully they've received the telephone call they've been awaiting for months. So make your visualizing as vivid as you can. What you are doing is impressing your mind.

Feeling has the same effect on your mind that someone running up to you on the street crying "Help, help!" would. If this happened you'd immediately drop everything and try to help. Your mind does the same thing. When you generate strong feeling with your visualization, you send out an urgent appeal to your mind which will pull out all the stops to deliver what you want.

Results Come as Opportunities

Your mind delivers in three separate ways. It delivers through opportunities of things you can do to have what you want. It delivers through spontaneous changes and it delivers by people offering things to you. It does this immediately. The fun of visualizing is taking up your opportunities.

For instance, if you're short of money you'll get a hunch about how to make some. If you want companionship, you may get an urge to take a night course where you'll meet someone. If you want to lose weight you may discover you're thinner even though you haven't been dieting. Out of the blue a relative may ring you up and offer you money. This happens all the time when people visualize. Or you may get invited to the theater, be invited on a trip or offered a used baby carriage!

About These Techniques

Some of the techniques in this book you'll relate to quite naturally—like driving a new car, or jogging in the park. Others such as living under a lucky star, turning back the clock, winning at cards, or exploding an irritating colleague may seem extravagant to you. Both have their uses. Some people relate better to scenes they can actually see happening in normal life. Others find fantasy techniques most effective. You'll probably enjoy a mixture of both. You'll be doing long visualizations and short visualizations. The long ones, like jogging in the park or visualizing your lifestyle goals you'll do once per session. Short techniques like acing serves at tennis or hitting the pad at a fun fair take only seconds to complete and are best visualized three times in succession in order to impress your mind.

Also, you'll find that certain techniques and examples given in later chapters seem at first to be concentrating on women or men. For instance Chapter 4, "Visualizing for Good Looks," takes women as its example, but the techniques are equally relevant to men. Chapter 5, "Visualizing in Business," and Chapter 6, "Destroy What You Don't Want," may seem on the surface to be angled toward men, but they are equally relevant to women.

Your Finest Computer

Some people wonder "How will seeing myself winning at cards help me close a deal?" You can trust your mind to put two and two together, it's the most advanced computer there is. When you visualize for a particular goal, you tap into a deep level of consciousness where change takes place. Some people call this your subconscious mind or your unconscious mind. On this level your mind has no idea of right or wrong. It only understands direction. When you lead your mind in a winning direction, for example by visualizing yourself winning at cards, or turning back the clock in order to achieve a particular goal, you impress your mind with winning for that particular goal, even if the technique has a lot of fantasy in it.

If, on the other hand, you visualize yourself losing at cards, you could put the kiss of death on your success by leading your mind in a direction of failure.

Is Visualization the Same as Hypnosis?

Some people think creative visualization is hypnosis, but there's a vast difference between them. Hypnosis is a superficial manipulation of your mind, and while it may temporarily help you give up smoking or overcome a phobia, very often your problem will crop up in some other form.

Studies have shown that when hypnotised people are asked to submerge one of their hands in a bucket of freezing cold water but are told it is warm they feel no discomfort. Yet when they're asked to write about how the water *really* feels with their other hand, they inevitably write words like, "Ouch," "It hurts," or "Take my hand out." So even under hypnosis you know when you're pretending.

Creative visualization is different. It goes to the very core of you—your heart—and changes the way you *feel*. It changes the way you feel about life, the world and the people around you. Most importantly it changes the way you feel about yourself and helps you realize you deserve the best.

Is Visualization Mind Over Matter?

Not really. "Mind over matter" implies the control or domination of something that's out to get you like a bad cold, flu, exhaustion, or noisy neighbors.

Visualization is a much more creative process. You are not suppressing anything when you visualize, you're creating. "Mind *re-educating matter*," might be a better way of putting it because when you're visualizing you are re-educating your body to be slimmer, your bank account to be larger or your relationships to be happier.

Why Visualize?

Learning to visualize will bring you more good luck than you can imagine right now. More specifically, it will do three main things for you.

Firstly, it will put you in the driver's seat. You're creating what you want instead of waiting *forever* for someone to give it to you. You'll experience a self-confidence and control you may have never felt. This doesn't mean that other people won't do things for you anymore. In fact you may be amazed at how they go out of their way to help you once you start visualizing. You're simply making it happen in your imagination first.

Secondly, visualizing will make you aware of the unlimited opportunities available to you. Sometimes they will be right under your nose. When you see how much you can do, it can be a little overwhelming at first.

Thirdly, visualizing will open you up to the unexpected. These are the mouth-watering windfalls everyone wants. Life is not all hard work, you can get lucky too. *Showing you how to have it easily is what this book is all about.*

The Enemy

Your only enemy when it comes to visualizing is your ego. Your ego is doubt, self-doubt. It's that voice that whispers in your ear when you're trying to accomplish something important: you should be replacing a burnt-out light bulb, playing with the children or washing the dishes.

When you're pushing to make an appointment it will

tell you that you forgot your mother's birthday. When you're dieting it will tell you "Go on, one piece of chocolate cake won't hurt you." It will dig up the past and say "Those were the good old days, too bad they're over." Your ego points out your mistakes, it blames, it shakes your confidence and makes you feel you don't deserve. Getting rid of the enemy through creative visualization is a process you'll really enjoy.

Planning Your Routine

How often should you visualize? I usually recommend one good session of about twenty minutes a day. You may think this is a lot, but when you experience what visualizing does for you, you won't want a moment less. Make a list of your goals to refer to when you're visualizing. It's also important to practice your techniques at a time of the day when you have good physical energy, so you may want to visualize first thing in the morning when you're fresh. Just before you drop off to sleep you can choose your favorite technique to visualize. Some people find this works better than a sleeping pill to insure you a good night's sleep.

Drive your car as if it's the new car you want

CHAPTER THREE

Create What You Want

You're always right about what you want. You want what you want and you should have it. It goes without saying your motives are fair. But to have what you want, you need to create it first in your imagination.

Decide what you want and *relax* into a comfortable position. You can sit in your favorite chair, curl up in bed, stretch out on the grass or sit under a tree. Some people take a few deep breaths and count slowly from ten to one to relax, others listen to soft background music, still others prefer complete silence.

Let's say it's money you want. How would you spend your money if you had it? What does your lack of money stop you from having right now? Close your eyes and *visualize* the thing you would buy if you had plenty of money.

Perhaps it's a new car you want. Imagine yourself going into the showroom and putting the cash for your new car on the salesman's desk. See the surprise on his face as he quickly hands you the keys. Hear them jingle in your hand as you walk over to your new car, open the door and get in.

Smell the new smell of the upholstery, run your hand over the seats. Hear the click of the seat belt as you settle in. In your imagination turn the key in the ignition and hear the sound of the new engine turn over. Now take a drive that you would normally take. Open the sun roof in your imagination, listen to the car's stereo, hear the sound of your children's laughter or your dogs barking as you drive your new car. Make this scene as vivid as possible.

When you *come out* of your visualization, *affirm,* "I, now own the new car I want" or something similar. Affirm this often as you go about your daily routine, and *act as if* it were true. When you drive your present car, even if it is a battered old rust heap, treat it *as if* it were the car you presently own. "See" your new car parked outside your house.

By carrying out this imaginary process on a regular basis, subtle changes will begin to occur in your life that will lead to your goal. Out of the blue you may be offered work that will finance your car. You may get a hunch to sell something that could give you the money. You may want to contact a friend or relative who can help you in some way. You might enter a lottery. You can do all of these things.

If your visualizing is to work, you must *follow through* with your hunches, because these are the steps that will lead to your goal. This is when your mind and your imagination come together to provide the solutions. Visualizing alone won't give you what you want, you need to *act*.

Visualizing for Health

Don't wrestle with your physical problems, no matter how severe they are. Use your imagination to jump over them. What does your problem stop you from doing right now? This is what you need to do in your imagination. Decide on a scene that could *only occur* if you were well. Let's say you have difficulty walking. This is where you need to relax, close your eyes and imagine yourself running!

Imagine you are jogging in a lush green park at the beginning of the day. Capture the feeling of running, feel the wind in your face, the dampness of your track suit, the springy trainers on your feet. Taste your sweat. Greet other joggers as you pass and collapse at the end of your jog and drink a cool glass of fruit juice. The more vivid you make this scene the better.

When you come out of your visualization and affirm, "I've just had a run in the park, and I feel great." Now act as if you had. Take a shower the way you would if you'd just come in from a run. If you've been using crutches you may feel like using them less, if so follow through with your hunch and try to get by without them more. When you do use them, affirm, "I am using my crutches less and less, and walking better all the time."

Through this imaginary process you'll get hunches about how to get well. You may feel like taking up yoga, having some physiotherapy like flotation, or taking a course of vitamins. Some people find that taking up a new hobby absorbs their attention so much that their physical problem completely disappears.

If you follow through with your hunches, you can get well. There are countless cases of cancer, MS, ME, HIV and infertility that have been reversed through creative visualization, often when nothing else has worked. It also resolves everyday headaches, backaches, fatigue, weight problems and other disorders. Orthodox medicine increasingly acknowledges creative visualization as one of the most powerful healing tools available today.

Live Under a Lucky Star

Everyone wants to be lucky. We see people who are. They always get what they want and never have to make much effort to get it.

People with good luck live under a lucky star. You can too. Visualizing a lucky star over your head will help you feel special and lucky. Close your eyes and visualize a bright star over your head, imagine its light permeating every cell of your body from the top of your head to the tips of your toes. Experience your feeling of wonder of knowing you're becoming lucky.

Now come out of your visualization and affirm, "I live under a lucky star and everything's going my way." This won't be difficult to do, because of the special feeling this technique generates immediately.

The good thing about lucky star techniques is that you can easily visualize them all day long. When you're driving your car visualize a star over your head, before an important appointment see it there, drop off to sleep under it. You can change the color and size of your star to suit your mood, and visualize lucky stars over other people in your life or your pets to keep them healthy and safe.

Deal Yourself a Winning Hand

Being American I love to play poker. It's the card game you see cowboys playing in Westerns. There are many different poker games but the one I enjoy most is five card stud with nothing wild. There are usually about five players and the one with the best cards wins. Someone with three of a kind could win, or two pairs, such as a couple of tens and a couple of threes. But the ultimate is to get a royal flush. This is the kind of hand that happens once in a lifetime, if ever. It beats four of a kind even if they're aces.

When I win with my royal flush I visualize myself sitting at a round card table with a green baize top. There are other players at the table and it's dimly lit except for a light over the table. We've been playing for a while and then I lay down my cards, an ace, king, queen, jack and ten in either diamonds or hearts. I "hear" a stunned silence as all the other players "fold" one by one. This is when they turn over their cards to show they are beaten. Then I pull in the "pot," a massive pile of money in the center of the table.

This kind of a visualization helps me to win in almost any situation. But it's especially useful when I have been working on a project I want to complete with style.

Aces Up Your Sleeve

There's another technique using the card game scenario which is helpful for making contacts, selling people on your ideas or succeeding in any way. It's having aces up your sleeve. Visualize yourself sitting at the same card table and when your turn comes around pull an imaginary ace out of your sleeve. Lay it face up on the table, then pull another ace out, and another and then the last. See the four aces face up on the table. Feel the speechless silence of the other players. See them "fold" and then pull in your pot of money. Enjoy the pleasure knowing the win is all yours because of the aces you had up your sleeve.

Visualize yourself slender and toned

CHAPTER FOUR

Visualizing for Good Looks

What you see in the mirror is very important to you. If you like what you see, you feel attractive and cheerful and things go your way. If you don't, you can snap at your children, suspect your partner, smoke too much, drink too much or criticize others to boost your morale.

Most women agree that growing older and losing their looks is a difficult area to deal with. This can affect men too. But it need not be so. You can stay looking good if you maintain your appearance, but you don't always do this. Why?

The main reason you don't maintain your appearance is because you *undervalue* yourself. You believe your ideas are silly or substandard and that you don't have much to offer. The result is that you feel depressed, not good for much and you let yourself go.

It's Never Too Late

There is nothing that can't be changed, if you find a battered old kettle in a flea market, you can renovate it, smooth it out and polish it until it's a gleaming feature of your home. The same holds true for a wooden table you fix up and wax until it glows. Sounds like plastic surgery? You can go for this if you want, but there are less barbaric ways of looking good. And less expensive to say the least.

When you bought the kettle and the table you "saw" something in them, beaten and worn as they were. You saw potential for beauty. You have this, too, but you have to bring it out in yourself. Creative visualization will bring out your good looks as nothing else will.

Glow With Happiness

Firstly, it cannot be emphasized too strongly how important a role your happiness plays in how you look. Every woman can be radiantly beautiful if she allows herself to have what she wants, and every man can be immensely attractive. It's the denial of your deepest desires that creates ugliness and tension. Unhappiness is the worst toxin there is.

So your most important "good looks" visualizing technique every day is to visualize yourself living the lifestyle you want, and following through with the actions that will make it happen.

Visualizing your lifestyle goals, such as a house in the country, setting up your own business or writing poetry, will take your attention from your problem and focus it on the solution. You'll have a vision. Not in an airy fairy way, but in the concrete way of something you want that you're creating. And you'll look good.

Your face will take on a clarity and glow. Your eyes will become clearer, you'll need less sleep, yet still look fresh. Others may say, "What have you been doing with yourself, you look so well." These are comments you can expect when you start visualizing regularly. You will literally glow from the feeling of happiness visualizing gives you. Both men and women experience this.

Correct Physical Faults

More specifically, creative visualization can help correct physical faults caused by age, illness or traits you've inherited from your family. There are endless problems visualizing can help solve, from weak fingernails, sallow skin, bad posture, to thinning hair.

This chapter will deal with the two most common problems: overweight and lines.

Mental Diet Makes Dieting Easy

A most effective visualizing technique for slimming down and firming up is to visualize yourself in a scene that could *only occur* if you were slender and toned. For instance lounging in a swimsuit by the sea. While the techniques that follow relate to people who want to slim they are equally effective if you want a fuller figure, or a more powerful body.

Relax, close your eyes and visualize yourself stretched out on the beach wearing a smart swimsuit. Feel the warmth of the sun on your skin, hear the sound of the surf and the distant laughter of other bathers. Feel a soft breeze blowing and capture your feeling of pleasure at being able to lie out in the open with the body you want.

In your imagination now picture every part of your body in turn. Start with your feet and see them trim and tanned. Next your slender ankles; next move up your calves and thighs and see them tanned and toned. Visualize your torso exactly as you want it to be. Move up to your neck in your imagination; if you are a woman you may enjoy seeing it longer and more slender than it is in reality. If you're a man you may like seeing it more powerful and strong. Admire your arms and hands, and lastly, imagine your face, radiant with self-confidence and contentment at finally having the body you want. As a last scene, visualize yourself *after* your day at the beach, playing squash, dancing, dining under the stars or walking in the moonlight.

Affirm Your Good Looks

This is a powerful visualizing technique. When you come out of it you may feel like you've been around the world! You have. You've just completely transformed your self-image. If you feel a little overwhelmed, give yourself a minute or so to "come to," then affirm, "Every day in the every way I am achieving a better looking body, I am happier and happier and more and more attractive."

Now go about your daily routine and act as if this were true. How would you walk, talk on the telephone and treat other people if you had the looks you wanted? How would you eat? Would you grab something on the run, or wolf down your food? How would you spend your day? Would you dine out with friends, start a career, settle down and have children or travel? To the best of your ability act like the person you have just visualized in your imagination.

Subtle Changes

What will happen next are three things. Firstly, your figure will start changing subtly of its own accord, but you may think you're imagining it at first. You'll get glimpses of yourself in the mirror looking thinner, or you may find that your clothes button up more easily. How this is possible will be explained at the end of the chapter.

If you want your visualizing to work, you need to accept these subtle changes and congratulate yourself for making them happen. If you brush them off and tell yourself "It's only my imagination," you'll undo all of your good work.

Secondly, you'll probably lose your appetite for foods that work against your looks, like chocolates, potato chips or heavily fried meals. They just won't appeal to you anymore. You'll probably prefer eating foods that will help you shape up like salads or fruits. You could lose your appetite completely. If so, check it out with your doctor and drink fruit juice for a day or so.

Thirdly, you're going to get ideas of things you can do to help your new figure along. You may get an urge to start swimming regularly, jogging, or bicycling to work. Everyone's way of shaping up is different, but your mind knows what will work best for you. If you follow through with your hunches you'll start achieving the figure you want *without the strain of dieting or the depression of denying yourself food.*

Go Shopping

You may long to wear clothes that your present figure would never allow. But in your imagination you can. Going shopping is a powerful visualizing technique to help make this happen.

Relax, close your eyes and imagine you're shopping in a smart store. Select your favorite clothing from the racks, try them on and see how beautifully they fit. Make sure you notice the sizes marked on the tags. If your present size is a sixteen, see a smaller size like a fourteen or twelve printed there. As a last scene visualize yourself on any occasion that appeals to you looking slender and smart in your new clothes. Feel the pleasure of looking good in the size you want. Come out of your visualization and affirm, "I can now wear the clothes I have always wanted to wear" and act as if you are wearing them now, even if what you have on is a shapeless pair of jeans.

Erase Your Lines

Lines that mar your face can depress you and make you feel over the hill. While lines are often attractive on a man, they usually don't enhance a woman. One of the best line remover techniques I've come across is one you'll be learning for worry, and that is erasing. Decide on the lines that bother you most, relax, close your eyes and imagine you are erasing each line from your face, the same way you would a line drawn in pencil on a piece of paper.

You'll need to get the knack of this technique. You can do it in two ways. You can imagine you're erasing lines directly from your face or you can imagine you're looking at a picture of yourself, where the lines are drawn in pencil.

The second is the one I use. I visualize a picture of my face with all the lines drawn in pencil, then I take out an eraser in my imagination and erase each line I dislike from the "drawing" of my face, brushing off the bits of rubber as I go. Then I switch back to my "real" face and visualize all of the areas where the lines were, seeing the skin fresh and young looking.

Whichever erasing technique you use, you may want to leave some expression lines that make you "you." As a last scene visualize yourself looking radiant and unlined in a setting you enjoy. Hear others commenting on how well you look. Hear them saying, "I don't know how you do it, but you don't have a line in your face." Feel the satisfaction. Come out of your visualization and affirm, "My lines are much fainter than before and soon they will be all gone." You can have it. If a pair of leather shoes can be polished up and made lovely, so can your skin. Visualizing is your first step.

Follow Through

What will happen next is the same that will happen with your weight. Your skin will start changing subtly of its own accord. Also you're going to get hunches. If you have lines that mar your lips, or heavy frown lines, you may "see" yourself rubbing some oil into them like vitamin E or an aromatherapy oil. You may get a hunch to go on a diet, go easy on the milk products or try a new skin care range. If you follow through with your hunches you'll speed your progress.

Turn Back the Clock

Time can turn into an enemy when you get older, but you can get the better of it. A superb technique to rejuvenate is to turn back the clock. As part of your everyday visualizing routine, picture a clock, but instead of seeing the hands moving forward, see them turn back. You can turn your clock back forty-eight hours in one go and become a day younger each day instead of older. Or you can turn it back seven days in one go if you want to speed up results. When you come out of the visualization, affirm, "Every day in every way I am getting younger and younger" and feel the pleasure of knowing you are "beating the clock."

This technique will have the same effect on you the lucky star technique has. It will make you feel special and lucky. Most importantly you'll feel you're in control of the aging process instead of being controlled *by* it and you'll take on a sparkle others will notice.

Think Pink

Another technique to help soften lines will also improve the color of your skin and that is to visualize the color pink. Relax, close your eyes and see your face permeated with pink light. You can breathe this light in or simply visualize your entire face (neck, arms, legs) bathed in it. See every line, sag, bag and wrinkle dissolve in the light. The shade of pink you choose can be any you find pleasing. Hold the image of your face radiant with pink light as long as you can. Then come out of your visualization and affirm, "The color of my skin is clear and glowing and my lines are fading away."

Mirror, Mirror

Looking in the mirror for results will sabotage what you're trying to achieve. So you need to learn to avoid it. If you've been visualizing to get rid of lines, excess fat, or jodphur thighs, don't immediately run to the mirror to see if they're still there. You'll only reinforce your ego, which tells you that you can't get rid of them.

Your mirror will tell you all by itself how you are doing if you'll let it. When you least expect it you'll catch a glimpse of yourself looking better than ever and you'll wonder "Is that *me?*" Your inner respose here is critical and will tip your scale toward aging or rejuvenation. Even if you find it hard to believe that you look so good, affirm, "Yes it is!" and mentally pat yourself on the back for making it happen. You are creating a new self-image when you visualize, and when you catch glimpses of yourself looking good you must accept what you see.

How Does Visualization Work?

You may wonder "How can visualizing make my face or figure change stubtly of its own accord?" A physicist could tell you exactly how this works, but it would take pages of technical explanation.

In layman's terms the subtle, spontaneous changes you experience from your visualizing have to do with the cells of your body which are mostly empty space when examined microscopically. Physicists and medical doctors have discovered that each cell of your body actually contains a miniature blueprint on your entire body. And depending on what you believe—what you focus your attention on—the cells of your body are either healthy or unhealthy.

Imagine

To better understand this concept the following exercise may help you. For a moment, look around you and notice everything that is green. You'll probably notice many green objects wherever you are. A plant, a jacket, a sofa, shades of green in a painting. When you're satisfied you've noticed everything green around you, read the following paragraph completely through before closing your eyes and turning the page:

In a moment you are going to turn the page of this book without looking at the first sentence written there. At the same time you turn the page also close your eyes for a moment. When you are ready, open your eyes and read the first sentence written on the next page. Do this now.

Turn Page

Without taking your eyes from this sentence, describe everything around you that is blue.

You may draw a blank on blue objects and have difficulty remembering them. The reason you don't remember the blue things is because you weren't looking for them. You were only looking for green.

When you visualize you do the same thing. By only looking for—visualizing—the things you want, you stop noticing the things you don't want, such as lines, fat, sags and bags, and they go away.

Change Your Body

"But how can this make my face or figure change of its own accord?" you may wonder. Every instant millions of cells in your body are dying off and being replaced by new ones. "You change your body faster than you can change your clothes" says Depak Choppra, M.D., in his audio tape series MAGICAL MIND, MAGICAL BODY. He goes on to explain how you have a completely new liver every six weeks as well as a new set of taste buds. You have a new skeleton every three months and every four days the cells of your stomach lining are renewed. Every month you have a completely new skin.

One year from today every cell in your body will have been replaced by a new one. The problem is that you *believe* that your body is *wearing out* instead of getting stronger and more vital, and you will look a year older at the end of a year instead of younger.

Whereas if you believed the *reverse,* you could look and feel a year younger.

Because you believe your body is wearing out your cells respond accordingly. This is where visualization can work dramatically. When you visualize health, beauty, rejuvenation, happiness and so on, you give your cells a new message which they respond to *instantaneously.*

This is the change you see in the mirror that you think you're imagining. But you are not imagining it, it's real. You have just reprogrammed millions of cells in your body through positive visualization. You have created a younger, healthier blueprint in each cell. But if you don't accept the change you see, and pass it off as "only imagination," your cells will cooperate with this negative response and change right back again. It is essential if you want to rejuvenate to accept the best you see.

Let the deal fall in your lap

CHAPTER FIVE

Visualizing in Business

The best use of creative visualization in business is in
closing deals and improving inter-office relationships.
In my experience some of the people who benefit most
from creative visualization are business people. Once
they start visualizing they never look back. They're
able to close deals, get troublesome people out of
their offices easily and make key contacts. Most importantly, they can work less and achieve more—thus
having more time to pursue their hobbies and be with
their families.

One manager I coached said that creative visualization
had streamlined his productivity the way the technique of speed-reading had honed his reading skills.

Close the Deal With a Gift

Closing deals can be fraught with tension. "I got the
deal I wanted, I just wish I could have been nicer
about it," one client said. "Everything goes amicably
until we sit down to negotiate, then we think we

have to get nasty." This is a complaint I've heard time and again, yet everyone can win in a negotiation.

Giving *imaginary* gifts before you sit down at the negotiating table has an uncanny effect of making deals close smoothly. *Relax, close your eyes and imagine* that you are giving gifts to everyone involved in the negotiation. It's important to give each person the gift he most wants to receive, not what you decide he should have.

Wrap your *imaginary* gifts any way you want; they can be huge boxes beautifully wrapped, or tiny boxes containing something precious. In your imagination hand your gifts to each person and see the pleasure on their faces as they open their gifts up and beam with delight. See them look at you, thank you, and know they mean it.

Now accept their imaginary gifts to you. Open them up and feel your delight at receiving *much more* than you expected. Experience your pleasure. As a last scene imagine that the contracts are all signed and everyone is shaking hands. Hear the champagne corks popping, taste the bubbly wine and enjoy the feeling of camaraderie that the deal you wanted is now successfully closed.

The gift box technique is useful for any situation where you need to create good will such as staff meetings, one to one sessions, meeting people for the first time or any relationship issues.

Let the Deal Fall in Your Lap

You get a real buzz when business falls in your lap with little effort on your part. This is an image you can use to your advantage. Say you want to close a deal. How would you actually feel if the contract you wanted just fell in your lap already signed? You'd be astonished. It would be too good to be true. Things just don't happen this way. But in your imagination they can. By visualizing the contract you want signed and falling into your lap you can streamline the process of closing any deal.

Relax and get comfortable, close your eyes and imagine you're sitting in a chair. Feel something being tossed into your lap, look down in your imagination and see the contract you've been waiting for all signed and sealed. Capture the feeling of astonishment you would naturally feel if this happened. Hold this feeling. This technique is quick, easy and potent. Do it three times in succession. Then come out of your visualization and affirm, "The deal I wanted is all

signed and delivered and it was unbelievably easy!"
Now act as if you had just completed the deal
you want.

Find the Needle in the Haystack

There may be some reason you can't close a deal
you've been working on. This happens all the time in
business, you get right up to closing and negotiations
stall. It can happen with a house sale or a complex
negotiation.

Everyone involved may be giving reasons while the
deal can't go forward, but you know these are just
excuses. If you could just figure out the real cause,
you could remedy it. You can. Finding the needle in
the haystack is foolproof for this.

Relax, close your eyes and visualize a pile of hay. See
a needle gleaming in the hay within *easy reach*. In
your imagination, reach over and take the needle out
of the haystack and dispose of it. You can examine it
first if you want to, the way you would a problem,
but it's not at all necessary. Drop the needle by the
road, in the rubbish or off a bridge. Dispose of it in
any way you wish, just as long as you make sure

you'll never have to encounter it again. When you come out of your visualization affirm, "The obstruction is removed, and the deal I want is now closed."

Making Influential Contacts

Being well connected in business is essential if you want to succeed. This is an area where you can feel like an outsider looking in. You think that if you could just get to the man at the top and tell him your ideas, he'd go for them. In your imagination you can do just this.

Just remember that *you* are the most influential person in your life and what you're really doing is influencing yourself to associate with people who can help you achieve what you want.

Relax, close your eyes and imagine you're on the outside of a smart office looking in the window at a group of successful business people inside. In your imagination go to the door of this building, open it and walk into the room where these people are gathered. See them turn around and greet you warmly, feel them shaking your hand and slapping you on the back as if they had been waiting for you for a long time. Hear the warm greetings all around and feel the pleasure of being accepted.

Now what would the outcome of making these contacts be? Would the business be so good that you'd buy a new sports car? A home in the country? If so, as a last scene see yourself driving this car, or walking in the garden of your country home. Now come out of your visualization and follow through with your leads.

Pocket Those Keys

You can establish key contacts in another way. Relax and visualize yourself walking into a gathering of people, such as a business meeting, a dinner party, a concert or an open market. See people come up to you one after the other, greet you warmly and hand you a large golden key. Look down at the key in your hand and see the luminous shine of pure gold. Take your key and pocket it. You can collect as many keys as you want, they can be more or less the same size or you can have one huge one. Feel your pockets bulging with keys. Then as a last scene visualize the outcome of possessing these keys. Would it be a trip? Would you redecorate your home? Visualize yourself in the scenario that would naturally result from possessing these keys. Then come out of your visualization and affirm, "I have so many key contacts that nothing can stop me."

Sometimes you have to demolish

CHAPTER SIX

Destroy What You Don't Want

Clients are amazed when I teach them destructive creative visualization techniques. But once they understand how these work they enjoy them immensely. These techniques can be used effectively in business, in your personal life and for your health.

Firstly you need to understand that these techniques are completely safe. They won't boomerang on you. This is because you can't destroy anything real. You can't destroy the blue sky which is real, yet your life, like the sky, can become so clouded over with problems that you can't make sense of it. This is where techniques that act like thunder, lightning, wind, and rain can help clear up your problems. Because these techniques are so potent, you only have to use them a few times to get results.

They're also very healthy for you because you release a lot of your negative emotions such as anger, frustration and resentment *in private,* so that when you face your family, friends or business associates, you are relaxed and confident.

When you destroy something it's important to always replace it with something new. This is because when you destroy something you create an empty space where it was. If you don't fill the empty space in your imagination with what you want, you may unwittingly refill it with the old problem.

Imagine

- Close your eyes and imagine your worst problem.

- Destroy it in any way you want.

- Replace it with what you want.

- How do you feel?

Let's say you're being plagued by some fellow in your office who seems to work against you. If, despite all your efforts to reconcile the misunderstanding, he persists in being awkward, you may have to demolish him.

Remember: you can't destroy anything real. Underneath this difficult individual, there's probably a person who can be helpful and wants to be liked. You can't destroy this person any more than you can destroy the blue sky. But you can destroy his egocentric, non-productive attitude which he and everyone else will be better off without.

Relax your body and mind, and picture him in your imagination. You may want to picture him as a Frankenstein monster to give color to your technique. Now explode him by any means you wish. You can drop a bomb on him or dynamite him. Hear the explosion, see it, feel its impact and enjoy the sensation. Now affirm, "John is more cooperative and good-tempered than ever." To the best of your ability treat him as if he were.

This technique will put you in control of the situation and make you feel good. As you explode your opponent in your imagination, you'll feel you're doing something positive about the predicament, so even if he remains difficult, it won't bother you.

What will happen next will be one of three things: this individual will become more cooperative and his negative attitude will disappear; he may become increasingly awkward, and hang himself and move on to another position; or the two of you will have it out and come to an understanding which enables you to work together in a supportive way. Whatever happens, the end result will be the same: you will be happier and so will he.

Cut Through Your Red Tape

A more benign destructive technique is cutting through the red tape. It works especially well in business and will streamline any area of your life. Cutting through the red tape is effective for difficulties where you can't see a way out.

Let's say you're facing bankruptcy, but you want to turn your business around. You may have so many problems with your bank manager breathing down your neck, having to sack employees, reduced sales and a staggering overdraft that you can't see a way out. You want to make your business profitable again but you feel it's too late.

Cutting through the red tape will toss up solutions, and it's also fun to do. In your imagination take out a pair of scissors and cut through all of the red tape you can see. Keep cutting. You may want to see your red tape with words like bankruptcy, overdraft, or falling sales written on it the way wrapping paper ribbon sometimes has.

If you experience resistance in your red tape and it slips out of the scissors or refuses to be cut, you may have to get a pair of wire cutters after it. Imagine that the tape is made of the kind of metal that huge boxes are secured with. Take out your wire cutters and cut this metal tape, then cut the next strip and the next. Feel the satisfaction. Then replace this scene by seeing your business booming and profitable again. Affirm, "My business is back in the black, I have regained my self-respect, and everyone else respects me." Now act as if this were true.

Let Go of Your Tragedy

Techniques that destroy can work for any area of your life, even a tragedy. Something may have happened to you that has "ruined" your life. While outwardly you may not show it, inwardly you can't get over the trauma this event caused. The memory of a divorce, illness, bankruptcy or childhood difficulties sticks with you, stopping you from wholeheartedly enjoying your life. It has to go. To get rid of it you need to identify the problem; next you need to identify the end result of this problem.

Example

- If it hadn't been for _____ my life would have been totally different.

- If it hadn't been for _____ I could have made it.

- Because of _____ I cannot do, have, enjoy _____.

Relax, close your eyes and bring the memory to mind.

You may have more than one. Destroy it. You can burn it up, bomb it, pour it down the drain, or dump it in the rubbish. Make sure you enjoy the whole process. After getting rid of the memory replace it with what you want.

Another tactic may be more helpful. Because tragedies make people feel trapped, you may feel as if someone has put you in prison and thrown away the key. Yet you can get out of this prison. Imagine you're behind bars. Then see someone come up and hand you a large golden key. Take the key, put it in the lock, turn it, and open the door. See how easily the door swings open. Now walk out into the life you want. This can be green countryside where your friends are waiting; it can be the bright lights of a city where you wear smart clothes and dine out; or it can be a retreat in the mountains close to the sky. Whatever lifestyle makes you happy, walk into it in your imagination. For good luck you may want to bomb your prison after you've left it.

Undo Missed Opportunities

Missed opportunities sting and make you feel you aren't deserving. Let's say one of your parents died and you had to leave school and help raise your family.

Because you didn't have the kind of education you wanted, you feel you don't fit in with the people you want to be with. Your career, your lifestyle and your friends may be completely different than the ones you dreamed of having. What's more you feel it's too late to change. You've missed the boat.

You can undo the memory of your hard luck. That you had to quit school and support your family cannot be changed, but you can change the way you *feel* about it. Your imagination can now help you to make it in another way.

Relax your mind and body, close your eyes and "see" yourself running up to the pier just as a boat pulls away. Make sure that the boat you miss is a little dinghy. See another boat immediately pull up, but this time make sure it's a big ocean liner.

Let the sight of the ocean liner take your breath away. See the gangplank come down, a red carpet roll out, walk up it and sail away. You can embellish this scene with dinner parties, friends, games and endless enjoyments. You can meet the partner you've been looking for on this boat.

Come out of your visualizing and affirm, "My life

has turned out much better than I could have ever imagined" or something similar. Now to the best of your ability feel confident and lucky and follow through with your hunches.

Erase Your Worries

The first chapter explained how worry pulls you down. You can explode worry in your imagination or burn it up. But one of the most effective worry techniques I have come across is to erase it.

Relax and close your eyes. Visualize a large piece of thick paper, possibly the kind artists use. See the word "WORRY" written on it. Make sure it's written in pencil, the kind that erases easily. Now in your imagination take an eraser and rub out this word. Erase every trace of the word "WORRY" from your paper. Now write a new word like "Serenity," "Peace" or "Happiness" in its place *in ink* so it can never be erased. This same technique can be used to get rid of pain, whether you're experiencing emotional pain, like loneliness, or physical pain, like a bad headache.

When you come out of your visualization and go about your normal routine, you may be surprised at how much more relaxed you feel right away. This technique is quick, easy and is best done three times in succession.

Jump Over Worry

Sometimes you have real cause for anxiety. Someone you love can be ill, or you can worry about their safety. A good way to handle this kind of worry is to jump over it in your imagination to a happy outcome.

When my son travelled through Africa for a year and came up against every kind of problem from war, illness, robbery to just plain loneliness, this is how I handled my worry. When I started to worry, I sat down and visualized my son arriving at the airport at the end of his journey. I "saw" him pushing his luggage trolley and beaming with pleasure. We gave each other a huge hug and began talking nonstop the way people do when they've been parted for a long time. By visualizing this over and over when I started to get edgy, I was virtually free of worry for the entire year he was away.

Tool-Box Techniques act like insurance

CHAPTER SEVEN

Back Up Your Success

Creative visualization should never be work; it should
be fun and you can devise endless techniques of your
own to achieve your goals. Yet some of the techniques
you'll need are to back up your success. These are
quick, potent and easy to visualize winning images. I
call them Tool-Box Techniques. They act like insurance—by doing them you ensure that all your other
visualizing techniques will work.

Ace It

Images that mean irreversible success to you are good
Tool-Box Techniques. Doing a few of these at the end
of your visualizing session will make you feel extra-
confident. One of these is to ace a serve. When you
ace a serve in tennis you succeed in one shot, with no
possibility of a comeback from your opponent. In this
case your opponent is the negative pattern you are
acing out of your life.

At the end of your visualizing session, ace some

serves. You can do this once or four times to win the game. Toss the ball up, feel your arm powerfully connecting with it and slamming it home. Hear a resounding "whack" as you ace the serve into your opponent's court. See him go for the ball, then stop short because he cannot return it. You've aced it. Feel the satisfaction. This technique is effective before important meetings or telephone conversations.

Hit the Pad

Another technique everyone enjoys, including children, is hitting the pad. You've been to a fun fair where there's every imaginable kind of game. You may have tried hitting the pad with the huge wooden sledgehammer to test how strong you are. The ball goes higher depending on how hard you hit the pad. If your hit is so hard you hit the top, a loud bell goes off and you get a prize. You can do this in your imagination when you want to win.

Relax, close your eyes and imagine you are at a fun fair. Hear the carousel music, and feel the bustle of people. Walk up to the "strength test," take the sledgehammer and hit the pad as hard as you can. Hear a resounding "boing" as you hit the top. You may want to see the top burst off, you've hit it so hard. Next see yourself receiving a prize. Let it be what you want. See the smiling face of the gamemaster as he hands you your contract, your new home, your slender body, or your bulging bank account. Feel the elation of having won what you want.

Scoring a goal, hitting the bull's-eye, winning a race, or hitting a golf ball are effective back-up techniques. Some people like to imagine they are a Concorde aircraft taking off, making a powerful sweep upwards and never turning back.

Tool-Box Techniques are useful when you don't have time to carry out your normal visualizing routine. For a day or two you can employ these as a stopgap to sustain your feeling of optimism.

Visualize for Others

Clients are amused when I teach them "happiness techniques" for other people, especially those who are causing them trouble. Yet once they experience how these work they always do them. Happiness techniques give you a sense of buoyancy, and make you feel indifferent to any antagonism that is aimed at you.

A friend saw her jealous mother-in-law doing a dance.

She visualized her dancing the way Snoopy does in the comic strip "Peanuts." Over and over she "saw" her mother-in-law whirling around on Snoopy's dancing feet, smiling and grinning. The first thing she noticed was that her mother-in-law telephoned less. My friend continued her visualizing. One day her mother-in-law announced her plans to visit friends in Canada, where she subsequently met a man and remarried. Her mother-in-law now has a life of her own and they visit from time to time without a vestige of the old jealousy.

Another friend saw a different dance. She visualized her depressed father-in-law so happy he was dancing a jig. Over and over she "saw" him kicking his heels, turning somersaults, and rubbing his hands with delight. The result was that she didn't react as impatiently to him as usual and he also became happier and more easygoing.

Happiness techniques bring you good luck because they bring about a subtle change in your attitude. When you visualize for others you go beyond yourself and become more receptive to opportunities "out there."

Catch a Star

"Catch a falling star and put it in your pocket, never let it fade away" is a song Perry Como made famous.

Using this image can help you a lot in your visualizing, so when you get good results, you don't let them *"fade away"* when your ego says it's "only imagination." Every time something positive happens as a result of your visualizing, like making a contact, or getting a promotion, take a minute to visualize yourself catching a falling star (your good luck), and putting it in your pocket. This will anchor your success and make you receptive to more. See your pockets or handbag bulging with stars.

Keep a Journal

It's invaluable in backing up success to acknowledge what you've already achieved. Every day you'll see signs that your visualizing is working. This can be something big like a job offer, or something small, but big to you, like your husband taking out the rubbish without your asking. If you write your successes down in a journal at the end of the day, it will give a real boost to your confidence. Some people call this their "good things" journal, their miracle list, or simply their diary. They say that writing out their successes actually helps them to *see* that their visualizing is working.

Keep your head in the clouds and your feet on the ground

CHAPTER EIGHT

Going Forward

Incredible things happen when you begin to visualize. Even hardened cynics experience this. For a start you'll achieve your goals more consistently, but the greatest benefit you may experience from creative visualization is the way it puts you in touch with yourself. What you are in touch with is your own power to create. After visualizing for a short time, you'll realize that there's nothing to stop you from having what you want. You're in the driver's seat and you'll feel good.

Keep That Sense of Timing

One of the most valuable effects of learning creative visualization is the acute sense of timing it will give you. You need this.

Timing is everything in life. If you do the right thing at the wrong time, it probably won't work. If you arrive too late for a train, you waste time and energy waiting for another. It's the same with opportunities.

67

If you don't seize the opportunity when it's ready, you have to wait for another chance. Creative visualization will give you the precise ideas you want and will show you exactly when and how to carry them out so as not to miss these opportunities.

Your Reaction Has to Go

There's one thing that throws a wrench into your timing and that is your *reaction* to people and events. When you react, your timing goes haywire. For instance, if someone accuses you of something, even if you didn't do it, your mind can go all over the place. You mentally defend yourself, you get angry and indignant, you decide to "get back," or you may sit down and try to figure out why this has happened to you. This all takes time and energy. The result is that you're thrown off your stride. You can lose a day, a month or even a year in turmoil before you get back on the beam of what you want. To succeed, you've got to be intelligent about how you use your energy. Creative visualization will make you impeccable in this.

One of the most beneficial techniques you can do as part of your visualizing routine is to destroy your reaction. You can visualize the word "REACTION" on a piece of paper and erase it, you can throw it on a fire and burn it up or you can put it in the rubbish. By getting rid of it, you'll find you're a lot steadier and consistent in creating what you want.

Use Your Down Time

You'll be doing one good visualizing session a day, but you can visualize at other times too. When you're stuck in a traffic jam, held up at the dentist's or sitting on the train, do some visualizing with your eyes open. You can put on dark glasses if this makes you feel more comfortable.

Techniques like erasing your lines, cutting through the red tape, happiness techniques, or other Tool-Box Techniques are useful here. Or you can catch the ocean liner. You might enjoy acing some serves while you wait for a business appointment. Each technique has the added advantage of encompassing the feeling of your other techniques, so by doing one you are in effect doing them all.

Let Everyday Routine Support You

Turn your everyday life into visualization. There are many things that you do every day that are automatic to you. Use these as visualizations. When you throw out the rubbish, in your imagination toss out your worry or your reaction at the same time. When you vacuum the carpet imagine that you are vacuuming up all of your fear. When you put on face cream imagine that you are massaging away all of your lines. Let sags, bags, illness and poverty drain out with the bathwater.

By becoming conscious of your everyday actions and giving them a positive new meaning, you can make immense strides.

Breathe in Success

Another everyday action you can turn into a visualization anytime, anywhere, is something you are already doing. You breathe. When you're waiting for an appointment or shopping for food, visualize what you want written in the air in front of you. For instance see the words "slender," or "rich," or "happy" written there, then breathe them in. When you breathe out see images of "fat," "poor," or "sad" leave your body and disintegrate into thin air. This technique will give you added energy as well as a sense of relaxation.

Results in Stages

Results come in stages. The first thing you'll notice when you visualize is that it will put a spring in your step.

You'll also notice coincidental changes in your life. Friends may invite you out more than before, or the reverse can happen if what you need is some space. You may feel like going on a diet, taking up physical exercise, or enrolling in a night course. You may get a sudden inspiration about how to make more money.

If you want your visualizing to work, you must act on these subtle changes because they are ushering in bigger changes that are on the way. Don't be disappointed that they are not the "big thing." Your mind and your imagination are coming together to provide you with solutions. Steps may be small at first. The reason for this is that you're waking up to opportunity. If you take advantage of the small opportunities, your mind will waste no time in giving you a chance to take a huge leap.

Trouble-Shooting

Going forward with creative visualization is like living in two worlds. This takes skill. It can also take courage. You'll live in a world of dreams which you are consciously creating, but you'll also live in a world of the here and now which needs your attention. This is where you have to balance watching, waiting and acting to make what you want happen.

There will be times when your visualizing is so vivid

that it may put you in a daze. What you have been visualizing may feel *so real* to you that you'll think everything is done and that all you need do is sit back and wait.

This is a sign that you have connected very powerfully on a fundamental level of consciousness where changes take place. But don't be tempted to stop visualizing unless you are sure that it's the right course. Give yourself a break for a day or so to reorganize your thoughts, and replace some of your techniques with some new ones that are more appropriate. Then keep going forward with your visualizing, using all of your common sense to make the best of your everyday life.

When Your Visualizing Stalls

What do you do if some area of your visualizing doesn't work? This can sometimes happen. Much of what you visualize can come true, but you may get stuck for a while on an issue like money, relationships or career.

This is where you need to work on your deservability. Because this is the only thing that stops you: your feeling that you don't deserve to have what you want, that you should wait, or only get it after a struggle.

This feeling of not deserving is completely counter-productive to your happiness, but you can get clear of this limiting belief.

Every day as part of your visualizing routine, do a visualizing technique for deservability just as routinely as you would brush your teeth. If you do this consistently you can get clear of *any* blockage. This may become your most valuable visualizing tool.

The technique I enjoy most is visualizing "DON'T DESERVE" written on a piece of paper. Then I take an eraser out in my imagination, erase the words and write "I deserve the very best. And *a lot* of it." I write this in large clear letters *in ink,* and do the technique at least three times in succession, sometimes more.

If your visualizing continues to stall you may need to talk your block through with a friend or counselor. You probably won't need more than a few sessions if you continue to visualize together with any counseling you get.

Dry Spells

You may hit a dry spell with your visualizing and want to give everything up. You may feel you're mad to pursue this imaginary course and that you should put an end to your dreaming, be practical and act.

You can't do this. You need to keep your head in the clouds *and* your feet on the ground. That is, you need to continue to visualize and carry on your practical living. You may have to go against what is considered normal or logical by your family and friends. This is where you need to be discreet about what you're doing and stick to your guns. Don't talk about your visualizing, keep it to yourself. When you have made what you want happen, then you can talk about it all you want.

"No Guts, No Glory" was printed on the T-shirt of a young student I met at a seminar. It made a powerful impression on me because it is the same with creative visualization. You can have what you want, but sometimes you need guts to manifest it. If you persevere you can achieve what you want. It's only in hindsight that you'll see how your puzzle came together to create the success you wanted.

Life Is on Your Side

Happiness is having what you want and it's never too late to start. Whether you are sixteen or sixty you can have what you want. Others may tell you that you can't. But you can. They may tell you that you'd better play it safe. The only problem is that while you're playing it safe, you can feel you're on the outside watching other people have what *they* want. Why should you be different?

You can have what you want. Others have, often in the face of hardship; often when they were considered "over the hill." You don't have to endure hardship, and you don't have to struggle. You do need courage. But the only courage you need is to believe in yourself.

You can let your old self-image go

CHAPTER NINE

Your New Self-Image

Your self-image is what you think you are. It's also what you *think* others think of you. But remember, what you think others think of you will always be *your* opinion. The problem is that what you think you are and what you really are are two different things. It's as if you have two people in you. One says you are a good person who deserves a lot of life. The other says you are a write-off and that you should settle for second best. You have to choose which "you" to believe in.

By practicing creative visualization you can side with the you who can succeed and have what you want. You can turn your habitually hard luck around. The following journey in imagination will help you to do this. You'll identify your present self-image and change it for the new one you want.

Read slowly through this imaginary journey. It's a meditation. Let your imagination create as many sounds, feelings and scents as possible. Don't worry if you don't get clear images when you are doing the meditation; some people get their insights later on as they go about their daily routine. Repeat the meditation as often as you like to capture the feeling of your new self-image.

You can record this meditation on audio tape using your own voice in order to participate more deeply; or you can purchase a pre-recorded version from Touchstone Publications Ltd., which has been specially produced to combine deeply relaxing sound and imagery in order to transform your self-image on a deep level.

Journey in Imagination

Relax your mind and your body in any way that works for you. You can sit in your favorite chair and look out the window, you can listen to the sound of your breathing, or you can drink a glass of wine. Do anything you enjoy to become relaxed and at ease.

Now that you're relaxed, count down from ten to one, letting your eyes close naturally when they want to. With each descending number feel yourself relaxing into a deeper and deeper state of relaxation.

Now find yourself walking down a country road on a

warm summer day carrying a basket on your arm. There's a breeze blowing and you can hear the sound of the birds in the trees and of a river close by as it splashes over the rocks. As you walk along this road, you are going to go back in time to when you were very small, and you are going to remember all of the experiences that have made up your self-image, the one that you have of yourself today. And as you walk along this road you're going to change this old self-image to the new one you desire.

You may be surprised at how easily the memories flood back. When you recall the memories that made you feel life was good, put them in your basket and take them with you. You may recall some sad memories but you can leave them behind. You don't need them, they don't do your self-image any good and they're not the *real* you.

When you reach the end of this road, you're going to walk onto a bridge, where you're going to choose a new self-image for yourself, a self-image that is positive and hopeful. Now as you collect your memories, you may want to put the memory of your first bicycle in your basket, or the day you scored a goal, or the day when you received your first pet, or the time you acted in your school play. See how easily and neatly all of your happy memories fit into your basket, and feel how light and easy to carry they are.

As you collect your memories, you sense that your basket is getting very full and you can see a bridge drawing near that crosses over the river. You can hear the sound of the river splashing over the rocks, and the sound of the wind in the trees, and of the birds singing as you breathe in the scent of this wonderful day. The smell of the summer grasses, as the sun glints through the trees, gives you a heady feeling of newness and hope in your future as you walk onto this bridge.

Yet as you stand on the bridge, looking around at the beauty, something catches your eye. You look down and notice a piece of paper folded in your basket that you hadn't seen before. As you take it out and unfold it, you see that there's a word written on it. The word written on this scrap of paper is the self-image that up until now you have had of yourself. What is the word that is written there? Is it waiting, struggling, missed the boat, overweight or poor? Read the word on the paper now, or let the wind whisper it to you.

And now, just as you have left all of your unhappy memories behind, take this piece of paper and drop it in the river and watch it float downstream until it disappears out of sight, and know that as you do this your old self-image, whatever it was, is gone forever. Now as you stand on the bridge, decide what you want your new self-image to be. Think about it. Let the sun tell you, hear it carried on the wind, let the water whisper it to you, let the birds sing it to you. Listen, listen, listen. What is your new self-image? Is it loved, happy, free, married, successful, healthy? Could it be all of these things? Listen to your new self-image and sense a bird softly flying by and dropping a new piece of paper in your basket. Look down at this new piece of paper and see the word that is written on it. This is your new self-image. Tuck it safely in your basket together with all of your happy memories. And now, when you are ready, walk off the bridge into the new life that awaits you on the other side. And remember that you can come back here any time you want, as often as you want, to reinforce the new self-image you have chosen for yourself today.

Tapes recorded by Julia Hastings can be ordered from Touchstone Publications, P.O. Box 57, Haslemere, Surrey, GU27 2RW, U.K.

You've got what it takes

CHAPTER TEN

Take Over the Conversation!

Positive affirmations help you sustain the positive effects of your visualizing. By repeating positive phrases that mean success to you, you crowd out the negative mental conversations you hold with yourself. It's the same as if you were trying to carry on a conversation with someone who talked nonstop. If you couldn't get a word in edgewise you'd eventually just stop talking and listen. This is exactly what affirmation does for you; it takes over *your* conversation. Instead of letting your ego tell you you're a write-off and that you've missed the boat, positive affirmation will tell you you're doing great, to go for it, and that you deserve the best life has to offer.

Affirmation is a good way of reprogramming your mind. When you're waiting for an interview, shopping at the supermarket or driving your car, repeating your affirmations silently or aloud will keep you bolstered up.

There are endless affirmations you can use. You'll

create many of your own. They'll just pop into your head. Many people find the following affirmation especially helpful.

"Every day in every way I am getting happier and happier, healthier and healthier and more and more successful." This will support you and help you succeed, whether you are trying to achieve a better figure, a more prosperous business or a happier marriage.

This affirmation has been adapted from one by Emile Coué: "Every day in every way I'm getting better and better." You can use Coué's version if you prefer, but people seem to get a stronger sense of resolve from the longer version. Say the affirmation that feels right to you, (saying the wrong affirmation is like eating food that doesn't agree with you or wearing a color that washes you out). The whole process of creative visualization, affirmation, and following through should be enjoyable and go with your mood.

Here are some more:

Happiness:

The more I give myself what I want, the happier I am.

Happiness (success, wealth, health, joy) is easy for me.

Happiness is the most important area of my life, and I now give myself everything I need to be happy.

I become happier every day.

I am having fun.

Luck:

I live under a lucky star.

I attract good luck.

Things turn out for me better than I can imagine.

My luck has turned around.

Everything I do brings me good luck.

Health:

Every day in every way I am getting healthier and healthier.

Life is on my side.

It's fun to be healthy and fit.

My good health has returned to me faster than I could have ever imagined.

I have left all my bad health behind.

Success:

The more I do what I enjoy, the more successful I am.

I always succeed.

I succeed at everything I attempt.

Nothing can stop me.

Everything is going my way.

Self-Image:

I am a unique and wonderful person. There is no one like me in the world.

I have released my old self-image and am now living my new self-image of happiness, success, companionship, health, wealth (and so on).

My positive, new self-image makes me happy and brings me good luck.

I have a strong powerful body, and a fine mind.

I am a good person. Nothing can stop me.

Good Looks:

I am good looking (beautiful, handsome, strong).

Aging is no longer a part of my life.

I am slender, toned and fit.

All of my lines are fading away.

Every day my body and face become better looking.

Deserving:

I deserve the very best life has to offer.

I'm always right about what I want and I can have it.

Anything I like, I can have.

I have let go of all my resistance to good.

I am as good as my best guest.

Life is on my side.